CULTURE
in the Kitchen

FOODS OF
Italy

By John Matthew

Gareth Stevens
Publishing

Please visit our website, www.garethstevens.com. For a free color catalog of all our high-quality
books, call toll free 1-800-542-2595 or fax 1-877-542-2596.

Library of Congress Cataloging-in-Publication Data

Matthew, John.
Foods of Italy / John Matthew.
    p. cm. — (Culture in the kitchen)
Includes bibliographical references and index.
ISBN 978-1-4339-5712-3 (pbk.)
ISBN 978-1-4339-5713-0 (6-pack)
ISBN 978-1-4339-5710-9 (library binding)
1. Food—Italy—Juvenile literature. 2. Cooking, Italian—Juvenile literature. I. Title.
TX360.I8M375 2011
641.5945—dc22
                                        2010049785

First Edition

Published in 2012 by
Gareth Stevens Publishing
111 East 14th Street, Suite 349
New York, NY 10003

Copyright © 2012 Gareth Stevens Publishing

Designer: Daniel Hosek
Editor: Therese Shea

Photo credits: Cover and all interior images Shutterstock.com.

Printed in the United States of America

CPSIA compliance information: Batch #CS11GS: For further information contact Gareth Stevens, New York, New York at 1-800-542-2595.

Contents

Words in the glossary appear in **bold** type the first time they are used in the text.

Oodles of Noodles and More!

Spaghetti, pizza . . . who doesn't love Italian food? Yet there are more kinds of Italian foods than those found in Italian restaurants in North America. People who visit Italy are often surprised to discover that meals can change so much from one town to the next.

For many years, Italy's mountains, hills, and other land features kept people from traveling easily from one place to another. Different **regions** became known for their special dishes using local **ingredients**. The result was a variety of delicious meals!

The beautiful regions and delicious foods of Italy attract millions of visitors each year.

▼

Italy

Europe

Pasta and Sauce

Pasta is an ancient food. Noodles made 4,000 years ago have been found in China. Records from around AD 100 report that Romans baked wheat noodles in ovens. Today, pasta in Italy is boiled in water.

Tomato sauce came much later. Tomatoes aren't native to Italy. Explorers brought tomatoes to Europe from North America. However, most people didn't eat tomatoes. They were afraid the red fruits were poisonous! Finally, in the 1800s, pasta and tomato sauce began to be served together.

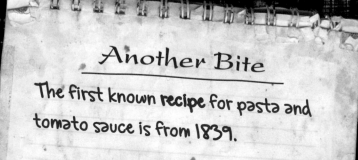

Another Bite

The first known recipe for pasta and tomato sauce is from 1839.

◀ There are more than 350 kinds and shapes of pasta, including spaghetti, linguini, ziti, and lasagna.

Homegrown and Homemade

Many Italian foods come from homegrown crops. Much of Italy has the right weather and soil for growing olive trees and tomatoes. Olive oil is just as important to Italian food as tomatoes. The two products are among Italy's biggest **exports**.

Though wheat is grown in Italy, so much pasta is eaten that wheat needs to be brought in from other countries, too. Most Italians eat about 50 pounds (23 kg) of pasta yearly!

But there's much more to Italy's foods than pasta and tomato sauce. Let's learn about Italy and its **cuisines**.

olive oil

Another Bite

Americans eat about 15 pounds (7 kg) of pasta each year.

The Italian word for tomato is *pomodoro*. The exact meaning of *pomodoro* is "apple of gold."

Northern Italy

Lombardy is a region in northern Italy. Pasta isn't as popular there as other grains. A small kind of rice is used to make a dish called risotto. **Polenta** is another popular grain. Meats, such as chicken, are first coated with bread crumbs and then fried. Dishes cooked this way are called Milanese, after the region's capital city of Milan.

To the east of Lombardy, the Veneto region touches the Adriatic Sea. It's known for seafood dishes.

Below these areas, Emilia-Romagna is famous for a thin, spicy ham called prosciutto.

Another Bite

The famous Parmesan cheese is named for the town of Parma in the Emilia-Romagna region of Italy.

◀ This creamy risotto dish includes porcini mushrooms.

Central Italy

Tuscany is a farming region. Olives, homemade cheese, and fresh **herbs** are common ingredients there. Soups made with beans are also popular. The city of Florence has many specialties. The phrase *alla Fiorentina* means "in the style of Florence." Bistecca alla Fiorentina is a recipe for high-quality beef served rare.

Some of the Umbria region's mouthwatering dishes are made with gnocchi (NOH-kee), which are potato **dumplings**. In one popular dish, gnocchi with ricotta cheese are baked with spinach in a tomato sauce.

◀ Gnocchi are often served with a sauce. These gnocchi are covered with four kinds of cheeses.

Foods of Rome

The city of Rome is found in the Lazio region of central Italy. Famous dishes there include spicy pasta arrabbiata. Pasta carbonara is made with eggs, pork, and cheese. Perhaps the most well-known dish is bruschetta. Bruschetta are thick slices of bread that are toasted, rubbed with garlic, and sprinkled with olive oil and salt. Sometimes tomatoes are placed on top. Artichokes prepared *alla Romana* (or "Roman style") are cooked in oil, garlic, and parsley. Artichokes are a commonly used vegetable in Italy.

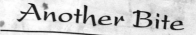

Another Bite

Arrabbiata is Italian for "angry." The chili peppers in the arrabbiata tomato sauce make it spicy.

bruschetta

Carbonara is from the Italian word for "coal." This pasta's name may come from the bits of pepper sprinkled over the dish that look like tiny pieces of coal.

The Invention of Pizza

Modern pizza began in the city of Naples in the southern region of Campania. In 1889, the people of Naples, called Neapolitans, wanted to prepare something special for their visiting queen. Queen Margherita was presented with a pie-shaped bread topped with foods the same colors as the Italian flag. The herb basil was the green topping. Mozzarella cheese was the white topping, and tomatoes added a red color. Today this pizza—the first modern pizza—is called a Neapolitan, or margherita, pizza.

Another Bite

Long before the queen visited Naples in 1889, different cultures around the world had been making flat breads and putting oil and herbs on them.

A true Neapolitan, or margherita, pizza uses mozzarella from the milk of buffalos. It also has San Marzano tomatoes. These are grown on plains south of Italy's Mount Vesuvius.

Sicily

Sicily is an island at the "toe" of boot-shaped Italy. The food there is different from Italy's other cuisines. This is because many different peoples have occupied Sicily over the years, including Greeks, Spaniards, Arabs, and even Vikings. Each left behind a bit of their own cuisine.

Many Sicilian pasta dishes include seafood from the surrounding waters. A common dish called arancini doesn't have pasta. It consists of balls of rice and meat coated in bread crumbs and fried. This recipe is over 1,000 years old!

Another Bite

Antipasto means "before the meal." Antipasto is the first course of an Italian meal. It may include meats, cheeses, vegetables, or any other food.

Arancini are called the "jewel" of Sicilian cuisine.

Desserts

Italian desserts are as tasty as the main dishes. Cannoli are fried, tube-shaped pastries that are filled with sweet cheese. These first came from the city of Palermo on the island of Sicily. Another sweet treat is gelato, or Italian ice cream. Naples is the birthplace of this creamy mix of milk, sugar, and fruit. Biscotti are popular cookies that are baked twice. Roman soldiers ate biscotti over 2,000 years ago! Tested by time, Italian food is truly some of the most delicious in the world.

cannoli

Recipe:
Homemade Pasta

(requires the help of an adult)

Ingredients:

1 egg, beaten

1/2 teaspoon salt

1 cup all-purpose flour

2 tablespoons water

Directions:

1. In a bowl, mix the flour and salt. Pour the egg in the middle. Mix until the **dough** is stiff. If needed, stir in 1 to 2 tablespoons of water.

2. On a lightly floured surface, **knead** the dough for about 3 minutes.

3. With a floured rolling pin, roll the dough until it's very thin.

4. Use a knife to cut the dough into strips as wide as you'd like.

5. Dry the pasta noodles by hanging them for about 3 hours. Store the dry noodles in a tight container for up to 4 days.

6. When you're ready to eat, boil water and drop the noodles in. They should be ready in 3 to 5 minutes.

Glossary

cuisine: a style of cooking

culture: a group of people who share beliefs and ways of life

dough: a mix of flour and water

dumpling: a small ball of dough, sometimes with food inside

export: a good that is sold to another country

herb: a low-growing plant used to add a taste to food

ingredient: a part of a mixture

knead: to work with dough until it's smooth

polenta: yellow flour made from corn that is cooked with water and sometimes baked or fried

recipe: an explanation of how to make a food

region: a large area of land that has features that make it different from nearby areas of land

For More Information

Books

Goodman, Polly. *Food in Italy*. New York, NY: PowerKids Press, 2008.

Thomson, Ruth. *Italy*. Mankato, MN: Sea to Sea Publications, 2007.

Websites

The Italian Chef

www.italianchef.com/recipes.html

Check out links to some of the most loved Italian recipes.

Italy

kids.nationalgeographic.com/kids/places/find/italy/

Read about Italy and see more photos of life there.

Index